My Mercury Book

By Nicholas J. D. Sims

Copyright © 2023 by Nicholas J.D. Sims

All rights reserved. This book or any portion thereof may not be reproduced or used in any manner whatsoever without the express written permission of the publisher except for the use of brief quotations in a book review.

Once upon a time, in a faraway corner of the galaxy, there was a small and rocky planet called Mercury.

Mercury was the closest planet to the Sun, and it was named after the Roman messenger god.

Mercury didn't have any moons or rings like some of the other planets. But it did have some interesting features, like craters, mountains, and valleys.

Some of these features were caused by meteorites hitting the planet's surface, while others were formed by volcanic activity long ago.

Mercury was small compared to the other planets in our solar system, but it was still fascinating. It was a very hot planet because it was so close to the Sun.

In fact, it was so hot that it could melt metal!

But don't worry, you wouldn't want to go there anyway — it's not a very friendly place for humans.

Mercury was discovered by ancient civilizations, but it wasn't until the 20th century that we were able to study it more closely.

In 1974 and 1975, the spacecraft Mariner 10 flew by Mercury and took pictures of the planet.

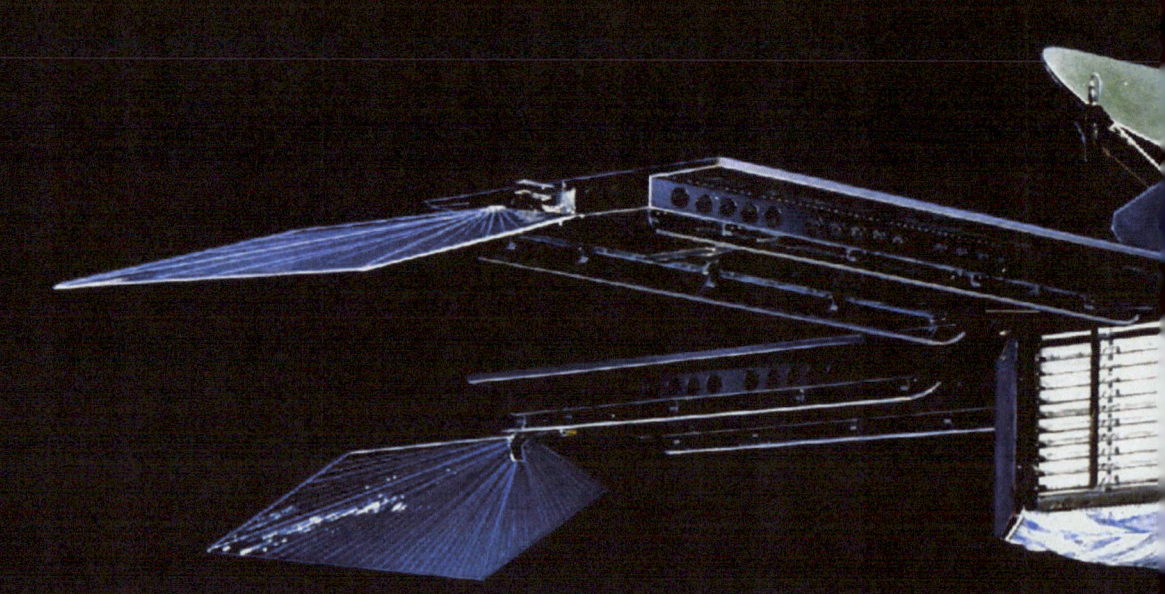

Then in 2011, another spacecraft called Messenger orbited Mercury for four years and sent back even more information about the planet.

Despite its hot and rocky terrain, Mercury still has lots to teach us about our solar system.

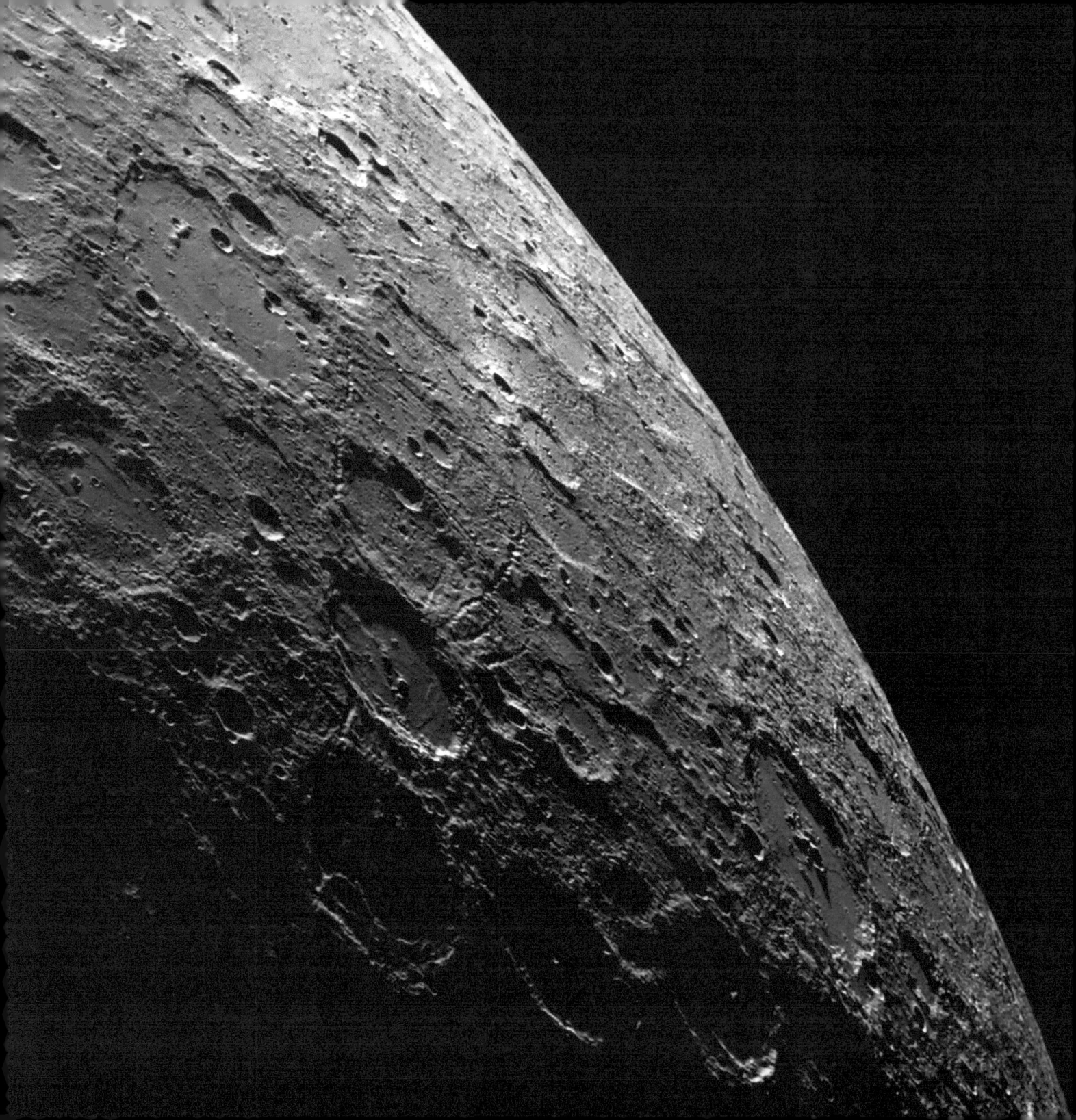

And who knows — maybe one day, humans will find a way to explore this fascinating planet up close.

The end.

ABOUT THE AUTHOR

My name is Nicholas Joseph David Sims. I am five years old. I have two dogs one named Mercury and the other named Bolt. Sometimes I call Bolt Venus as his nick name. My nick name is Nicholatte. My birthday is December 2nd, 2017. I started reading when I was two years old. I like to learn about the weather like tornadoes, earthquakes floods, and hurricanes. I want to be an Astrogeologists when I grow up. I really love science. I would like to thank my Dad and Mom for being the best parents in the world.

www.ingramcontent.com/pod-product-compliance
Lightning Source LLC
Chambersburg PA
CBHW042251100526
44587CB00002B/106